SWORD ART ONLINE
-calibur-

SWORD ART ONLINE Calibur
CONTENTS

ART: SHII KIYA
ORIGINAL STORY: REKI KAWAHARA
CHARACTER DESIGN: abec

HEY...

LOOK AT THIS, ONII-CHAN.

CHAPTER 1

WH-WHAT!?

MMO TOMMROW

VRMMO NEWS SITE

MMOトゥモロー

TOP ALO GGO GA

Latest News

ALO 2025.12.28 NEW!!

> The legendary weapon Holy Sword Excalibur, found at last!

HRRMM... SO THEY FINALLY FOUND IT!

HONESTLY, IT TOOK A LOT LONGER THAN I EXPECTED.

AWW, MAN...IF I'D KNOWN THIS WAS GONNA HAPPEN, I'D HAVE GIVEN IT ANOTHER SHOT...

はぁー

HAAA (SIGH)

READ IT CLOSER.

THEY ONLY JUST FOUND IT.

THEY HAVEN'T FIGURED OUT HOW TO GET IT YET.

HEE HEE!

OH, YOU'RE RIGHT...

MAN, DON'T SCARE ME LIKE THAT.

BUT HOW'D THEY FIND IT, THEN?

YOU CAN'T FLY IN JOTUN-HEIM...

...AND THAT SPOT IS SO HIGH, YOU CAN'T SEE IT WITHOUT FLYING.

PLUS, TONKY ONLY COMES WHEN YOU OR I CALL FOR HIM.

A YEAR AGO, ON THE QUEST TO ALNE...

ONII-CHAN!?

...WE GOT SWALLOWED BY A GIANT WORM WHICH EXPELLED US INTO THE UNDER-GROUND REALM OF JOTUNHEIM.

THERE, WE CAME ACROSS A JELLYPHANT DEVIANT GOD BEING ATTACKED BY A HUMANOID ONE.

ONII-CHAN!

LET'S SAVE THE ONE BEING PICKED ON!!

WE ALLIED WITH THE BEAST-LIKE DEVIANT GOD AND LURED THE HUMANOID ONE INTO THE LAKE...
...SO THAT OUR CHAMPION COULD WIN THE FIGHT IN THE WATER.
WE NAMED THE CREATURE "TONKY"...
...AND IT LATER GREW WINGS, TAKING LEAFA AND ME...
...UP THE PASSAGEWAY IN THE CEILING OF THE CAVERN THAT HEADED TO THE SURFACE.
BUT ALONG THE WAY, I SAW...
...RESTING AT THE BOTTOM OF THAT INVERTED PYRAMID DUNGEON...
...A GLOWING LONG-SWORD...

MAYBE SOMEONE ELSE SAVED ANOTHER JELLY-PHANT...
...AND SUCCEEDED IN ACTIVATING THE QUEST...?
SURE, I GUESS ......
BUT IT'S HARD TO IMAGINE ANOTHER WEIRDO—

...ER, ANOTHER CHARITABLE SOUL SUCH AS YOURSELF WANTING TO SAVE SUCH A GROSS—
...ER, UNIQUE MONSTER LIKE THAT.
KWOO! ♥
PUKU (STEAM)
IT'S NOT GROSS! IT'S CUTE!

BUT IN THAT CASE, IT'S ONLY A MATTER OF TIME BEFORE SOMEONE CLEARS THAT DUNGEON...
ACK!
...AND SUCCEEDS IN RETRIEVING THE SWORD.

IT WASN'T DISCOVERED UNTIL NOW BECAUSE THE CONDITIONS FOR UNLOCKING THE QUEST WERE WELL HIDDEN...

...BUT IT'S BEEN A YEAR, AND THERE WAS THAT UPDATE THAT ADDED SWORD SKILLS...
...SO THE DIFFICULTY OF THE DUNGEON ISN'T WHAT IT ONCE WAS.

YEAH...... I GUESS ......

YOU DOING ANYTHING TODAY, SUGU?
...WELL, THE CLUB'S ON BREAK.
I'M PRETTY SURE SEVEN IS THE MOST YOU CAN FIT ON TONKY'S BACK.
THAT MEANS ME, YOU, ASUNA, KLEIN...
...LIZ, SILICA... AND ONE MORE.
AGIL'S GOT HIS BUSINESS.
CHRYSHEIGHT IS TOO UNRELIABLE.
RECON'S GONNA BE IN SYLPH TERRITORY...
WHY NOT INVITE SINON-SAN?
OOH!
THAT'S IT!

LISBETH ARMORY, CAPITAL CITY OF ALNE
ARE YOU ALREADY ON NEW YEAR'S VACATION, KLEIN-SAN?
Silica
Cait Sith
Pina
Feathery Dragon
YEP, SINCE YESTER-DAY.
EVEN IF I WANTED TO WORK, THERE'S JUST NO BUSINESS THIS TIME OF YEAR.
AND THE STUPID BOSS TRIES TO SPIN IT BY SAYING THAT WE'RE A WORKER-FRIENDLY COMPANY!
HEY, KIRITO, IF WE ACTUALLY MANAGE TO STRIKE GOLD AND WIN EXCALIBUR TODAY...
...YOU GOTTA HELP ME GET THE SPIRIT KATANA KAGU-TSUCHI.
Klein
Salamander
GUI (NUDGE)
AW, MAN... THAT DUNGEON'S SO FREAKIN' HOT.
YEAH, AND JOTUNHEIM'S SO FREAKIN' COLD!
IF WE'RE MAKING REQUESTS, I'D LIKE THE BOW OF LIGHT, SHEKINAH.
Sinon
Cait Sith
YOU MADE YOUR CHARACTER TWO WEEKS AGO, AND YOU'RE ALREADY AFTER A LEGENDARY WEAPON ......?

THE BOW LIZ MADE ME IS WONDERFUL...
...BUT I COULD USE A BIT MORE RANGE...
JUST SO YOU KNOW!
BOWS IN THIS WORLD ARE BASICALLY SOMEWHERE BETWEEN SPEARS AND MAGIC SPELLS IN TERMS OF RANGE!
Lisbeth Leprechaun
YOU CAN'T NORMALLY USE THEM TO HIT A TARGET A HUNDRED YARDS AWAY!
IF I COULD, I'D GO FOR TWICE THAT RANGE.
GUI
OF COURSE, YOU CAN ALREADY HIT LONG-RANGE TARGETS WITHOUT ANY SYSTEM AIM WITH YOUR LONGBOW.
I CAN SEE HOW YOU WERE AN ELITE SNIPER BACK IN GGO*.
*GUN GALE ONLINE
GACHA (CLICK)
WE'RE HEEEERE!
THANKS FOR WAITING!
...WE WERE GATHERING SOME INTEL ON OUR SHOPPING TRIP...
Leafa Sylph
Asuna Undine

IT SEEMS LIKE NO PLAYERS OR PARTIES HAVE REACHED THE HANGING DUNGEON YET.

THAT'S GOOD NEWS FOR US, PAPA!

Yui
Navigation Pixie

REALLY? BUT IN THAT CASE...

...HOW DID ANYONE DISCOVER EXCALIBUR'S LOCATION?

Kirito
Spriggan

APPARENTLY, THEY FOUND ANOTHER QUEST...

...SEPARATE FROM THE TONKY QUEST WE CLEARED.

AS A REWARD FOR THAT OTHER QUEST...

...AN NPC POINTED OUT WHERE EXCALIBUR COULD BE FOUND.

AND IT SOUNDS LIKE THIS OTHER QUEST WAS PRETTY VICIOUS.

IT WASN'T AN ERRAND QUEST, BUT THE SLAUGHTERING KIND.

JOTUNHEIM IS PRETTY DECIMATED, WITH PEOPLE FIGHTING OVER POP SPOTS.

YEAH... THAT SOUNDS MESSY...

DON'CHA THINK IT'S WEIRD?

EXCALIBUR'S SEALED AT THE VERY BOTTOM OF A FLOATING DUNGEON...

...PACKED WITH TERRIBLE MONSTERS, RIGHT?

WHY WOULD JUST THE LOCATION ITSELF BE A QUEST REWARD?

THAT'S A GOOD POINT.

I WOULD UNDERSTAND IF THE REWARD WAS THE MEANS OF GETTING TO THE DUNGEON, BUT...
WELL, I'M SURE WE'LL FIND OUT WHEN WE GET THERE.
ALL RIGHT! EVERYONE'S WEAPONS ARE AT FULL CAPACITY!
THE WAIT IS OVER!
ガチャ GACHA (CLANK)
THANK YOU VERY MUCH!
HEY, GUYS!
THANK YOU FOR ANSWERING MY ABRUPT SUMMONS TODAY.
I'LL PAY YOU BACK FOR YOUR ASSISTANCE—MENTALLY!
AND NOW... ...LET'S KICK SOME ASS!
YEAAAAH!!!!!!!

...SO THIS IS TONKY'S SECRET TUNNEL, HUH?
HE TOOK US UP HERE AFTER WE SAVED HIM.
YIKES... HOW MANY STEPS ARE ON THIS THING?
ABOUT THE LENGTH OF AN ENTIRE LABYRINTH TOWER FROM AINCRAD.
UGH... THIS SUCKS...
LISTEN, IF YOU WANTED TO GET TO JOTUNHEIM VIA THE NORMAL ROUTE...
...YOU'D HAVE TO TRAVEL TO A STAIRCASE DUNGEON MILES FROM ALNE...
...FIGHT MONSTERS ALL THE WAY DOWN...
...THEN DEFEAT A BOSS AT THE END—JUST TO GET HERE.
IT'D TAKE A SINGLE PARTY AT LEAST TWO HOURS TO DO THAT, BUT THIS IS JUST FIVE MINUTES OF WALKING!
EEEESH!
SO DON'T COMPLAIN! LET GRATITUDE FILL YOUR HEART...
...FOR EACH AND EVERY STEP OF THESE STAIRS, BOYS AND GIRLS!
HEH.
YOU TALK AS IF YOU BUILT THEM.
POSO (MUTTER)
GRR!
SORO (SNEAK)

THANKS FOR THE FEED-BACK.
GIU (CLENCH)
BIKU (JUMP)
FGYAAAA!?
TH-
THE NEXT TIME YOU DO THAT!
BUN (SWIPE)
BUN
BUN
I'M SHOOTING A FIRE ARROW UP YOUR NOSE!
HE'S FEARLESS...
AT LAST...
...WE REACHED THE FROZEN CAVERN OF JOTUN-HEIM...
...AND WITH THE HELP OF TONKY THE JELLY-PHANT...
...WE TOOK OFF FOR THE ENORMOUS DUNGEON THAT WAS THE HOME OF THE LEGENDARY BLADE...

ONII-CHAN, LOOK AT THAT!
FROM ABOVE, WE SAW...
...A THIRTY-MEMBER RAID PARTY WITH THE VICIOUS HUMANOID GIANTS...
...WORKING TOGETHER TO ATTACK AND SLAUGHTER TONKY'S FELLOWS.
WAAAAA (CHEER)
THE HUMANOID DEVIANT GODS ARE HELPING THEM...?
WHY AREN'T THEY FIGHTING THEM?
SHUUUU (FSHHH)
...!
THE ANSWER TO THAT QUESTION CAME TO US...
...IN THE FORM OF A MYSTER-IOUS, BEAUTIFUL GIANT.
SHE'S— HUGE!

I AM URD, QUEEN OF THE LAKE.
LITTLE FAIRIES WHO HAVE ALIGNED YOURSELVES WITH MY KINDRED...
...MY TWO SISTERS AND I HAVE A REQUEST OF YOU.
PLEASE SAVE THIS LAND FROM THE ATTACK OF THE FROST GIANTS.
...KIN-DRED?
TONKY?
KWOO?
LIKE YOUR ALFHEIM, JOTUNHEIM WAS ONCE UNDER THE BLESSING OF YGGDRASIL, THE WORLD TREE.
WE HILL GIANTS LIVED HERE PEACEFULLY WITH OUR KINDRED BEASTS.
CLEAN WATER FLOWED THROUGH OUR STREAMS, AND LUSH GREENERY ABOUNDED.

BELOW EVEN JOTUNHEIM...
...LIES NIFLHEIM, THE REALM OF ICE.
ONE DAY, THRYM, KING OF THE FROST GIANTS...
...TURNED HIMSELF INTO A WOLF AND SNUCK INTO JOTUNHEIM.
HE CAST THE SWORD THAT CUTS ALL STEEL AND WOOD, EXCALIBUR, FORGED BY WAYLAND THE BLACKSMITH GOD...
...INTO THE SPRING OF URD IN THE CENTER OF THIS WORLD.
THE SWORD SEVERED THE WORLD TREE'S MOST VITAL ROOT...
...AND IN THAT MOMENT, JOTUNHEIM LOST THE BLESSING OF YGGDRASIL.
A GREAT HORDE OF KING THRYM'S FROST GIANTS SPILLED FORTH...
...FROM NIFLHEIM INTO JOTUNHEIM.
THEY ENSLAVED WE HILL GIANTS...
...AND BUILT THE CASTLE, THRYMHEIM, OUT OF THE BLOCK OF ICE THAT WAS ONCE MY SPRING.

MY SISTERS AND I SURVIVED AT THE BOTTOM OF A SPRING THAT FROZE OVER...
...BUT OUR FORMER POWER IS LOST.
HOWEVER, THE FROST GIANTS WERE NOT SATISFIED WITH JUST THAT...
THEY CONTINUE IN THEIR ATTEMPTS TO WIPE OUT OUR KINDRED BEASTS, WHO STILL SURVIVE HERE.
!
IF THEY SUCCEED, MY POWER WILL BE ENTIRELY LOST...
...AND THE CASTLE THRYMHEIM WILL BE ABLE...
...TO ASCEND...
...INTO ALFHEIM ABOVE.
WH-WHAT!? BUT...
...THAT'LL TOTALLY DESTROY ALNE!
KING THRYM'S GOAL IS TO LOCK ALFHEIM UNDER ICE AS WELL...
...AND INVADE THE BRANCHES OF THE YGGDRASIL TREE...
...WHERE HE WILL FIND THE GOLDEN APPLE THAT HE SEEKS.

ANGERED BY THE CONTINUED SURVIVAL OF OUR KINDRED BEASTS, THRYM AND HIS FROST GIANT GENERALS...
...HAVE DECIDED TO USE THE STRENGTH OF THE FAIRIES TO ACHIEVE THEIR GOALS.
THEY PROMISE EXCALIBUR AS THE REWARD...
...TO CONVINCE YOUR PEERS TO HELP SLAUGHTER OUR KINDRED.
BUT THRYM WOULD NEVER GIFT THAT SWORD TO ANOTHER.
IF EXCALIBUR LEAVES THE CASTLE THRYMHEIM...
...THE BLESSING OF YGGDRASIL WILL RETURN TO THIS LAND...
...AND HIS CASTLE WILL MELT INTO WATER ONCE MORE.
SO... EXCALIBUR BEING A REWARD IS ALL JUST A LIE!?
WHAT KIND OF QUEST IS THAT!?
I BELIEVE THAT WHEN WAYLAND THE BLACKSMITH GOD FORGED THE BLADE...
...HE MADE ONE IMPURE STRIKE AND CAST ASIDE HIS FAILURE.
I SUSPECT THRYM INTENDS TO GIVE AWAY THE FALSE BLADE, CALIBURN...
...WHICH IS OTHERWISE INDISTINGUISHABLE FROM EXCALIBUR.
IT IS VERY STRONG ON ITS OWN BUT DOES NOT CONTAIN THE HOLY SWORD'S TRUE POWER.
N-NO WAY! HE'S A KING, AND HE'S JUST GOING TO LIE ABOUT THAT...?

THAT CRAFTINESS IS THRYM'S GREATEST WEAPON.
BUT IN HIS HASTE TO WIPE OUT MY KINDRED BEASTS...
...HE MADE ONE MISTAKE.
IN ORDER TO HELP THE FAIRIES HE TRICKED WITH HIS HONEYED WORDS...
...HE SENT MOST OF HIS FOLLOWERS FROM THRYMHEIM ...
...DOWN TO THE SURFACE BELOW.
RIGHT NOW, HIS CASTLE'S DEFENSES ...
?!
KYUIIIIN (KWEEENG)
OH!
...ARE BUT A SHADOW OF THEIR NORMAL STRENGTH.
WHEN THE FACETS OF THIS MEDALLION ARE ALL BLACKENED AND DARK...
...THAT IS WHEN ALL OF MY KINDRED ARE DEAD ...
... AND MY POWER IS GONE FOR GOOD.
FAIRIES, WILL YOU INFILTRATE THRYMHEIM...
...AND DRAW EXCALIBUR...
SHUOOOOO (WHOOSH)
...FROM THE KEYSTONE PEDESTAL?

...I THINK WE HAVE NO CHOICE, ONII-CHAN.
I AGREE. AFTER ALL, I GATHERED YOU HERE TODAY...
...SO WE COULD TACKLE THAT DUNGEON AND GET EXCALIBUR.
IF THEIR GUARD IS DOWN, EVEN BETTER.
WAIT FOR US HERE, TONKY!
WE'RE GONNA MAKE SURE...
...YOU GET YOUR REALM BACK!
GOOOOO (WHOOSH)

GOOOOO
THIS IS A STICKY SITUATION, ONII-CHAN!
THE GOLDEN ONE...
...HAS TOO MUCH PHYSICAL RESIS-TANCE!
GIRI (CLENCH)
NUHOOO (LOOM)
ONE!
TWO SECONDS TO SHOCK-WAVE!

ZERO!!!
DODOO (KABOOM)
HNG!

KIRITO-KUN!
AT THIS RATE ...
...I'M GOING TO RUN OUT OF MP IN 150 SEC-ONDS!
GOOO (VWOOM)

DAMN!
KIIIIN (VEEN)
AT LEAST WE CAN HURT THAT ONE, BUT THEN...
THE BLACK MINO'S RECOV-ERING AGAIN!
...THE GOLDEN ONE STEPS IN!
THE GOLDEN MINO-TAURUS HAS EXTREME PHYSICAL RESIS-TANCE.
GIIN (CHING)
YAAAAH!!
DAAAA!!
KIIN (TING)
WITHOUT MUCH MAGE POWER...
...WE CAN'T KNOCK ITS HP DOWN ENOUGH!
AND EVEN WORSE...
WE CAN DODGE THE DIRECT ATTACK...
YEOW, THAT'S CLOSE!
BO (FWOOM)
GOA (WHOOSH)
...BUT WE STILL TAKE SPLASH DAMAGE FROM IT!
UGH!

KIRITO-KUN!
KYUIII (KWEEE)
IF WE GET WIPED, WE'LL HAVE TO START OVER FROM ALNE...
... AND WE DON'T HAVE THAT KINDA TIME...
ONII-CHAN!
SHUUU (FSHHH)
THE MEDALLION IS OVER 70% BLACK NOW.
WE DON'T HAVE TIME TO DIE AND TRY AGAIN.
......
GOT IT.
GROAH!
DOO (BOOM)

SHE'S RIGHT ...
WE DON'T HAVE TIME...
EVERY-ONE!
DODOO (KABOOM)
THERE'S JUST ONE THING WE CAN DO!
ONE WAY OR ANOTHER ...
...WE HAVE TO BEAT DOWN THE GOLDEN ONE WITH CONCEN-TRATED SWORD SKILLS !!

SWORD SKILLS
A weapon technique far more powerful than normal attacks, that aids the player with automated movement assistance.
Advanced sword skills don't just do ordinary physical damage like normal attacks...
...but add magical elemental damage like fire, water, earth, wind, darkness, or light.
SO THIS SHOULD ENSURE THAT EVEN THE PHYSICAL-RESISTANT GOLDEN MINOTAURUS...
...WILL TAKE MAJOR DAMAGE.
HOW-EVER...
...THE MOVEMENT DELAY AFTER A SWORD SKILL IS LONG.
IF WE GET HIT BY THAT DEVASTATING AX...
EVERY MEMBER IN THE FRONT AND MIDDLE ROWS...
...WILL BE COMPLETELY OBLITERATED!!!

HELL YEAH!
THAT'S WHAT I'VE BEEN WAITIN' FOR, KIRI, MY MAN!

SILICA!
TA (TEK)
GIVE US BUBBLES ON MY COUNT!
BASA (FLAP)
OK!
GOAAA (ROAR)
DO (RUMBLE)
ONE!
...TWO!
DO
DO

NOW!!
PINA!
BUBBLE BREATH!!
POWAWAWAN (WUMWUMWUM)
PACHIN (BLINK)
PA (POP)
PA
!?
PACHIN
PA
GO!!
DAN (DASH)

HRNG...!?
NAA...
GOO (WHOOSH)
HAAAA!!

GA (CUT)
GA
BYUO (WHOOSH)
GA
GA
DO (BOOM)

GIRO (GLARE)
UM... UH-OH!
HURRY!
GOTTA GET OUT OF SKILL DELAY!
WE JUST PULLED AGGRO!
KIIN (TING)
KIRI (CRICK)

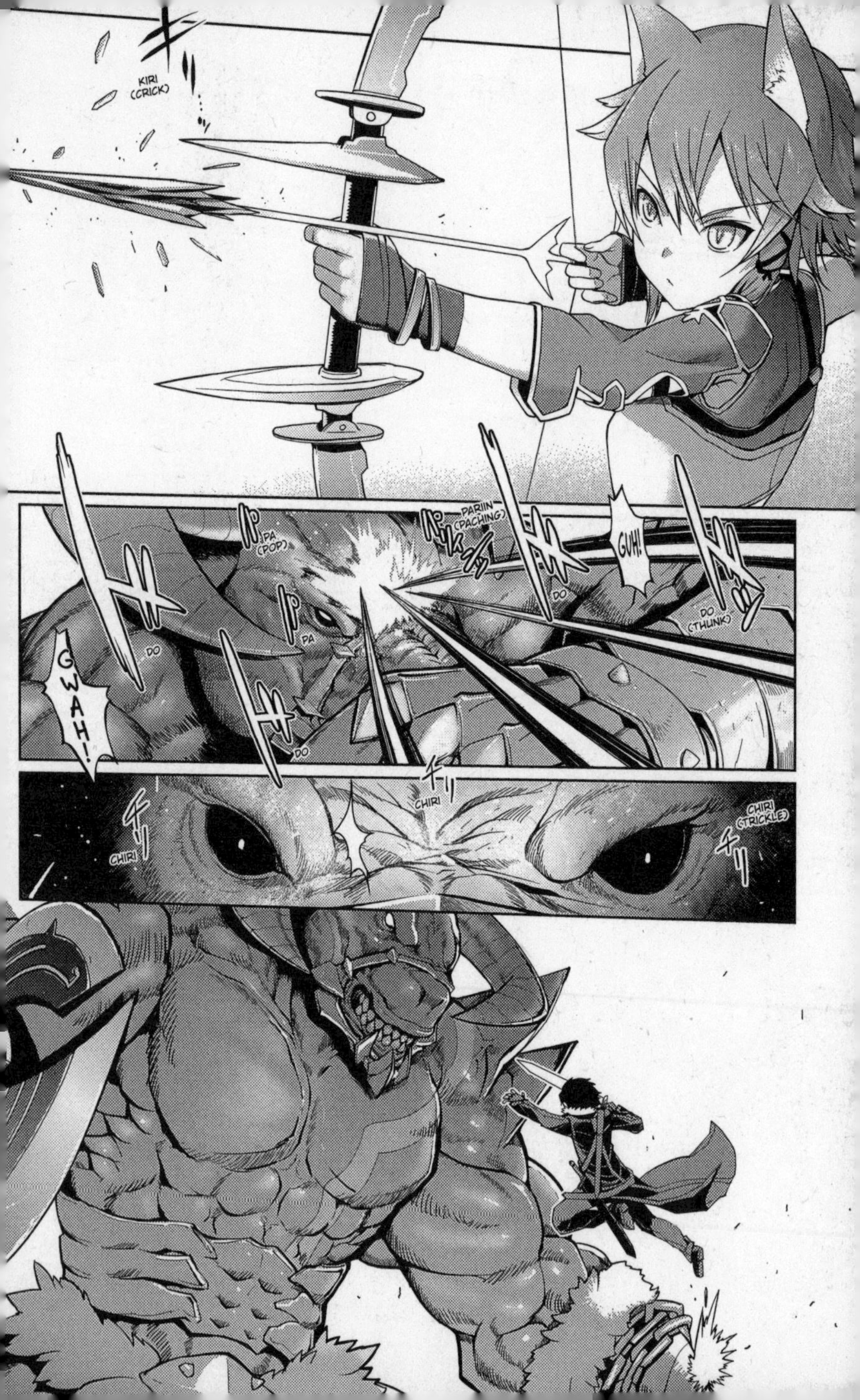
KIRI (CRICK)
PARIIN (PACHING)
GUH!
PA (POP)
PA
DO
DO (THUNK)
DO
DO
GWAH!
CHIRI (TRICKLE)
CHIRI
CHIRI

HAAAA!
DO
DO
DO
DO
DO
RRRAA!!
BA (HUP)
GUH...
BA
BO (FWOOM)
RAH!

PARII (PLING)
GOLDEN Minotaurus
IT DOES 40% PHYSICAL, 60% FLAME DAMAGE!
ONE OF THE BIGGEST ONE-HANDED SWORD ATTACKS!
NATURALLY, ITS SKILL DELAY...
...IS APPROPRIATELY LONG FOR ITS POWER...!
THE EIGHT-PART LONG-SWORD SKILL...
...HOWLING OCTAVE!!!

HOW-EVER...
...!!
WHAT I CAN DO NOW IS SEPARATE MY MIND ...
...FROM MY RIGHT HAND!
FOR JUST ONE INSTANT, I IMAGINE I'M CUTTING ALL BRAIN SIGNALS...
...GOING TO THE AMUSPHERE.
AND MY NEXT COMMAND ...
...IS TO JUST MY LEFT HAND!!

AAAAH!!
GAKYU (SHUNK)
HAH!
GA (THUNK)
WAIT... DUAL BLADES?
NO...
THERE ARE NO UNIQUE SKILLS IN ALO!

HOLY SWORD.
IMMORTALITY.
SYSTEM ASSISTANCE.
DUAL BLADES.
THESE IRREGULAR POWERS THAT EXISTED IN SAO...
...HAVE ALL BEEN SCRUBBED FROM THE SYSTEM BY NOW FOR ALO.
AND YET...
KURU (SPIN)
AT THE VERY LAST ACTION FOR "SAVAGE FULCRUM"...
I SWITCH AGAIN...
...AND GO FROM LEFT HAND...
YAA!

VUOOOON (VWOMM)
AAAA...
SHUNT BRAIN-POWER FROM ONE SIDE TO THE OTHER!
...TO RIGHT!
AAA!
THE WINDOW TO PULL OFF THIS TRICK...
...IS LESS THAN 1/10TH OF A SECOND!!!
YAAAAH!!
ZUDO (THWAM)

CHAPTER 2

BA (BAM)
GOLDEN Minotaurus
BA
BA
ALL RIIIGHT!
HERE WE GO...

DOOO (WHAM)
HEY ...!
NO PEEK-ING!
YAAAAH!
DODO (KABOOM)

AL-MOST THERE!
THERE'S JUST...
...ONE MORE ROUND TO GO!
GOLDEN Minotaurus
I'VE HARDLY EVER RUN A COMBO LONGER THAN THIS, EVEN IN PRACTICE.
BUT...
NI (SMIRK)
...!!
GOTTA GO FROM RIGHT TO LEFT ARM AGAIN.
AND MY MARGIN OF ERROR...
...IS ZERO!
AAH!
MAAAAH!

CONNECT!

LET'S...
...GO!
GOO
WAAAH!

GOOOO

...!
HE...
DOZAA (SKID)
HE DID ...
PIKOOON (DING)
GOLDEN Minotaurus
ZUN (LOOM)

GURURUUUU
(RUMBLE)
ZUOOOO
(ZWOOOSH)

YAAAAAH!

YOU OKAY, KIRITO-KUN?
I'M SURPRISED YOU MADE IT FROM THE BACK ROW.
NICE WORK.
KYUOOO (WHOOSH)
THANKS.

FULL...
BIKOOON (BING)
BLACK Minotaurus
...RECOVERY!
DAN (STOMP)

......AW-
RIGHT...
SIT YER ASS DOWN...
...RIGHT THERE, COWBOY.

HEY, KIRITO!
SINON-SAN...
WHAT THE HELL WAS THAT ABOUT!?
ガッ
GA (GRAB)
YOU BET YOUR ASS YOU DO! I'VE NEVER SEEN ANYTHING LIKE IT!
...DO I HAVE TO EXPLAIN?

IT'S A NON-SYSTEM SKILL OF MINE.
I CALL IT "SKILL CONNECTION."
OOOOH!
お〜〜っ
16 HITS IN TOTAL.
SINON WAS COUNTING?
WOW... WHY DO I FEEL LIKE I JUST GOT WICKED DÉJÀ VU?
ぽん
PON (PAT)
JUST YOUR IMAGINATION.
BUT THERE'S NO TIME TO SIT AROUND AND RELAX.
LEAFA!
HOW MUCH TIME DO WE HAVE LEFT?
OH, RIGHT.
...LOOKS LIKE WE MIGHT HAVE AN HOUR LEFT...
...BUT NOT TWO.

I SEE.
......YUI...
...YOU SAID THIS IS A FOUR-LEVEL DUNGEON?
にゅっ
NYU (PEEK)

YES. THE THIRD FLOOR IS ABOUT 70% THE SIZE OF THE SECOND...
...AND THE FOURTH IS ESSENTIALLY JUST THE BOSS CHAMBER.
1ST FLOOR
2ND FLOOR
[HERE NOW]
3RD FLOOR
4TH FLOOR
BOSS!
THRYMHEIM

THANKS.
なでり
NADERI (RUB)
なでり
NADERI
HEE HEE!

RIGHT NOW, ON THE MAP OF JOTUNHEIM BELOW...
...THE PLAYERS UNDERTAKING THE FROST GIANT FACTION QUEST...
...WILL BE PICKING UP STEAM IN THEIR EXTER-MINATION OF THE ANIMAL-TYPE DEVIANT GODS.

WE'LL BE LUCKY IF WE HAVE MORE THAN AN HOUR.

ASSUMING THE FINAL BOSS... PROBABLY THRYM HIMSELF...
...IS GOING TO TAKE A WHOLE THIRTY MINUTES TO FIGHT...

...THEN WE NEED TO CLEAR OUT THE THIRD AND FOURTH FLOORS IN THE OTHER THIRTY!

IF ONLY WE HAD A BIT MORE TIME...
WE COULD'VE EXPLAINED THE SITUATION TO THOSE PLAYERS DOWN THERE...
...AND MIGHT HAVE GOTTEN THEM TO GIVE UP ON THEIR QUEST...
OR WE COULD'VE CALLED SAKUYA AND ALICIA RUE FOR BACK-UP...NAH.
IT WOULD'VE TAKEN THEM UNTIL NIGHTFALL TO GET HERE ANYWAY.
OUR ONLY OPTION IS FOR THE SEVEN OF US...
...TO OVER-COME NEARLY IMPOS-SIBLE ODDS.
ALL RIGHT, THEN!
I DON'T KNOW MUCH ABOUT THIS DEVIANT GOD KING OR WHAT-EVER...
DON (WHAM)
...BUT IT SEEMS OUR ONLY CHOICE IS TO RUSH HIM AND WIN!
WHOA!
YEAH!!

HURRY, ONII-CHAN!

YOU CAN DO IT! ♡

ONCE ALL LEVERS ARE PULLED, WE HAVE TEN SECONDS...

THIS IS A WEIGHT-MEASURING PRESSURE POINT...

...FOR A SINGLE FEMALE AVATAR.

ニヤ NIYA (GRIN)

ニヤ NIYA

WHY ME TOO!?

I'M NOT HEAVY!

I SWEAR!

END OF THE 3RD FLOOR
WHAT THE...?
UM...
PLEASE......
FREE ME......
...FROM THIS PLACE......
...!

IT'S A TRAP.
BIIN (YANK)
ACK!
THAT'S A TRAP.
TOTALLY A TRAP!
GUKI (CRICK)
Y- YEAH... IT'S A......
... TRAP.
UM...... MAYBE?
CHIRA (GLANCE)
CHIRA
HMPH...
YUI?
SHE'S AN NPC.
LIKE QUEEN URD...
ANALYZE_
Type:Non Player Character
...SHE IS CONNECTED TO THE LANGUAGE-ENGINE MODULE.
...BUT THERE'S ONE DIFFERENCE.
THIS WOMAN... ...HAS AN HP GAUGE ENABLED.
NORMALLY NPCS HAVE THOSE DISABLED, BECAUSE IF THEY DIE, THE QUEST GETS STUCK.
※STUCK: WHEN AN ERROR PREVENTS THE QUEST FROM PROCEEDING PROPERLY.

DO DO
IF AN NPC HAS HP, THAT MEANS...
...IT'S THE TARGET OF AN ESCORT QUEST ...!!
DO (BADUM) DO DO
ENEMIES HAVE HP TOO.
ABSOLUTE TRAP.
DEFINITELY A TRAP.
I THINK IT'S A TRAP.

O-OKAY, IT MIGHT NOT BE A TRAP...
...BUT WE DON'T HAVE TIME FOR SOME TRIAL AND ERROR RIGHT NOW.
STOP WITH THE FACES.
WE'VE GOT TO GET TO THRYM AS SOON AS WE CAN.
RIGHT?

...IT'S A TRAP.
I KNOW...
...IT'S A TRAP.
...BUT...
KIRARI (GLINT)
...EVEN SO...
EVEN KNOWING...
H-HUH...?
YAWN!
IS HE GETTING EMOTIONAL OVER AN NPC...?
...IT'S A TRAP...
EVEN THEN, I CAN'T HELP MYSELF!
I CAN'T JUST LEAVE HER HERE!
EVEN IF...WE FAIL THE QUEST... AND ALNE IS RUINED...
...SAVING HER HERE IS THE RIGHT CHOICE...
...AS PER MY CREED—!
DOON (BOOM)

MY SAMURAI CODE!!
DA (DASH)
HEY!
I'M COMING TO SAVE YOU NOW!!
...!
WHAT AN AWESOME HERO...
GU (CLENCH)
......AND WHAT AN IDIOT.
WE DON'T HAVE TIME FOR THIS...

...THANK YOU, FAIRY SWORDS-MAN.
HEH...
CAN YOU STAND?
SU (SWISH)
ARE YOU...
LET'S JUST GO, GUYS!
... HURT ?
NO...
I'M FINE.
IT'S AN AWFUL LONG WAY TO THE EXIT.
CAN YOU MAKE IT THERE ALONE, MISS?
......

......I CANNOT SIMPLY ESCAPE FROM THIS CASTLE RIGHT AWAY.
I SNUCK IN SEEKING A RELIC OF OUR PEOPLE THAT THRYM STOLE FROM US.
BUT THE THIRD GUARDIAN SPOTTED AND IMPRISONED ME.
ZUI (LEAN)
I CANNOT RETURN UNTIL I HAVE THE TREASURE.
WILL YOU PLEASE ...
UH... YEAH ...
...TAKE ME TO THRYM'S CHAMBER WITH YOU?
SOMETHING ABOUT THIS SEEMS FISHY...
YA THINK ...?
H-HEY... KIRI, MY MAN ......
ALL RIGHT!
FINE, FINE...

I GUESS WE'RE STUCK ON THIS STORY ROUTE UNTIL THE END.
WE'RE NOT 100% SURE IT'S A TRAP, I SUPPOSE.
YOU'VE GOT A DEAL, MISS!
DIVERSITY MAKES FOR STRANGE BED-FELLOWS!
AND NOW, TO FACE THRYM AND RIP HIS BALLS OFF!
THANK YOU...
...SIR SWORDS-MAN!
DON'T GET YOUR SAYINGS MIXED UP, OR YUI WILL LEARN THEM.
LIKE SHIPS THAT PASS...
...ON THE RIGHT!
PI (BEEP)
NPC Participation
PI
MUGYU (SQUISH)
Asuna Hp Mp
Sinon Hp Mp
Freyja Hp Mp
"FREYA" ...? IS THAT HOW YOU PRO-NOUNCE THAT?
LOOK AT THAT MP...! A MAGE, MAYBE?
PIROROROn (BLIIING)

LET'S HOPE SHE STICKS WITH THE PARTY TO THE END...

LISTEN UP!

BASED ON THE CONSTRUCTION OF THE DUNGEON, THE FINAL BOSS'S CHAMBER SHOULD BE JUST DOWN THOSE STAIRS.

HE'S GONNA BE TOUGHER THAN THE OTHERS...

...AND WE HAVE NO CHOICE BUT TO FACE HIM WITHOUT ANY TRICKS.

FIRST, WE'LL FOCUS ON DEFENSE UNTIL WE GET A HANG OF HIS ATTACK PATTERN.

THEN I'LL GIVE THE SIGNAL TO FIGHT BACK.

WHEN HIS GAUGE GOES YELLOW—AND THEN AGAIN WHEN IT HITS RED...

...BE EXTRA CAREFUL. WATCH OUT FOR CHANGES IN HIS PATTERNS.

AND NOW...

...LET'S BLAZE OUR WAY THROUGH THIS FINAL BATTLE!

YEAH!!!!

SWORD
ART
ONLINE
—calibur—

CHAPTER 3
GOUN (GONG)
I'LL REBUFF ALL OUR STATUS EFFECTS.
PAAAAA (GLOW)
SO SHALL I.
SHUOOOO (SWOOSH)
!?
THAT'S A HUGE HP BOOST.
Kirito
Hp
Mp
IS IT A SPECIAL NPC SPELL?
GO (RUMBLE)
GO
GO
GO
Brace!!

ゴゥン
GOU (VMMM)
WHOA ......
WOW ......!
MOUN-TAINS OF TREASURE ...!!
OH MY GOSH...
HOW MANY YRD WOULD ALL OF THIS TOTAL...?
I COULD FRANCHISE MY LISBETH ARMORY WITH THIS!
THIS IS AMAZING.
NOW I WISH...
...I'D EMPTIED MY INVENTORY FIRST...

LITTLE BUGS ......
... FLITTING ABOUT...
I CAN HEAR THE BUZZING ...
...OF THEIR OBNOX-IOUS WINGS.
ゴフゥゥゥ
GOFUUUUU (FWOOSH)
I SUPPOSE ...
ビリ
BIRI
BIRI (RATTLE)
...!

DODOON (BOOM)
...I MUST CRUSH THEM...

...BEFORE THEY CAUSE TROUBLE!

HAH!

HAH......

INSECTS OF ALFHEIM...

...SUMMONED HERE BY URD'S PLEAS.

LITTLE ONES, IF YOU TELL ME...

...WHERE I MIGHT FIND HER...

GUFUUUUU (SNORT)

...YOU MAY TAKE ALL YOU CAN CARRY OF MY GOLD. WHAT SAY YOU?

...HEH!

POVERTY AND STARVATION ARE NOTHING TO A WARRIOR!

IF YOU THINK I'D JUMP AT A PITIFUL OFFER LIKE THAT, YOU'VE GOT ANOTHER THING COMING!

TCH.
AH-HA.
...OH-HO.
IS THAT YOU THERE, FREYJA?
SINCE YOU ARE OUT OF YOUR CAGE...
...I SUSPECT YOU MUST HAVE AGREED TO BE MY BRIDE AT LAST?
HMM?
...B—
BRIDE !?
INDEED.
THIS GIRL WAS BROUGHT INTO THE PALACE...
...TO BE MY BRIDE.
NUUUUUU (LOOM)

BUT THE NIGHT BEFORE THE CEREMONY...
...WE CAUGHT HER SNIFFING AROUND MY TREASURE ROOM.
I PLACED HER IN AN ICY CELL AS PUNISHMENT. HAH! HAH!

...SO FREYJA IS HERE...
...TO TAKE BACK HER PEOPLE'S STOLEN TREASURE.
SHE PRETENDED SHE WOULD BE THRYM'S BRIDE TO GAIN ENTRY TO THE CASTLE AND ITS TREASURE ROOM...
...BUT THEN GUARDS SPOTTED HER, AND SHE WAS CHAINED UP.

SINCE THAT CHECKS OUT...
...IT'S UNLIKELY SHE'LL BACKSTAB US IN A FIGHT.
BUT SOME-THING STILL DOESN'T ADD UP.

WHICH OF THE NINE FAIRY RACES IN ALFHEIM IS HER "PEOPLE"?
WHAT IS THE STOLEN TREA-SURE?

I SHOULD'VE ASKED THESE QUESTIONS WHEN WE RECRUITED HER...
KUI (TUG)
KUI

LEAFA?
I THINK I READ ABOUT THIS IN A BOOK...
ONII-CHAN.
THE STORY OF THRYM AND FREYJA ......
...AND A STOLEN TREASURE. LET'S SEE...
HOW DID IT GO?
WELL—
BA (WHOOSH)
WHO WOULD EVER MARRY YOU!?
WHOA!
INSTEAD, I SHALL BATTLE YOU WITH SIR SWORDSMAN AND HIS COMRADES...
...AND TAKE BACK WHAT WAS STOLEN!
BWAH!
HAH!
HAH!
GOOOOOO (WHOOSH)
HOW BOLD YOU ARE!

HAH!
THERE IS GOOD REA-SON...
HAH!
BWAH!
...TALES OF YOUR BEAUTY AND VALOR HAVE REACHED ALL NINE REALMS, FREYJA.
NITAA (LEER)
ZOKU (SHIVER)
...!
HOW-EVER ......
THE PROUDEST FLOWERS ...
...ARE THE MOST TEMPTING TO PICK...

ONCE I HAVE CRUSHED THESE FLIES...
...I WILL ENJOY SHOWER-ING YOU...
...WITH THE LOVE...
...YOUR BEAUTY DE-SERVES.
BWAH HAH!
HAH HAH HAH HAAH!
RERO (CLICK)
H—
HOW DARE YOU!!
H—
YOU'LL NEVER HAVE HER!!
EWW... WHAT'S UP WITH THIS BOSS ENEMY?
WHAT A CREEP...
BEARDO!!
MISOGY-NIST!!
...GO TELL HIM OFF FOR US, ONII-CHAN!
WH-WHY ME?

THE GREAT KLEIN-SAMA WILL ENSURE ...
...THAT YOU NEVER LAY ONE STINKING FINGER ON FREYJA-SAN!!
WELL, WELL!
I HEAR THE BUZZ-ING OF LITTLE WINGS!
GOON (KRUNCH)
LET US SEE NOW!

PERHAPS I SHALL FLATTEN YOU AS A PRE-CELEBRATION...
...TO MY CONQUEST OF ALL OF JOTUNHEIM!!!
Thrym
The King of the Frost Giants
Thrym
Hp
GOOO (VWOOM)
OOOO (WHOOSH)
LOOK AT ALL THOSE HP BARS!!
HERE HE COMES!
LISTEN FOR YUI'S ORDERS...
...AND REMEMBER, ONLY DODGING FOR THIS FIRST PART!

NRRR RNN GH!!
DOGOO (BASH)

HE STARTS OFF...
GOOO (VOOM)
...WITH A MAJOR ATTACK!?
IT'S A TYPE OF ICE BREATH!
OOO
THE WARM-UP MOTION IS BIG...
...SO WE SHOULD HAVE TIME TO WATCH FOR IT THEN DODGE!
BACK ROW, WATCH OUT FOR AREA EFFECTS!
FRONT ROW, SPLIT UP AND ATTACK HIS LEGS!
AT HIS SIZE, THEY'LL BE A BLIND SPOT!
JUST DON'T GET STEPPED ON!
KIIIIN (SHINE)
BWAH HAH!
ALL THIS FLIT-TERING ABOUT!
HOW-EVER—!
YOU WILL NEVER BE MORE THAN BUGS TO ME!

!?
BO
BO
BO (CHUNK)
BO
BO
WH- WHAT'S THAT!?
ARE THOSE...
...DWARVES MADE OF ICE!?
BWAH HAH HAH!
AN EYE FOR AN EYE...
...A BUG FOR A BUG!
LEAD THE ATTACK...
...MY ICE HENCHMEN!

CHAPTER 4
DO (STOMP)
DOO
DO
...!

KIRI
(CRICK)
AH!
AH!
KA
(TAK)
KA
KA
HOLY COW!
TWELVE ARROWS, ALL HEAD-SHOTS!?
NICE ONE, SINON!
CAN YOU HANDLE THE DWARVES ON YOUR OWN?
CER-TAINLY.
SUCHA
(SHWIK)
I'M ON IT.

GREAT! THEN LET'S...
... ATTACK ......
NUOOO (LOOM)
SO, UM...
WE'RE... AIMING FOR THE LEGS... RIGHT?
UM... YEAH.
I MEAN, UP CLOSE, NOT LIKE WE CAN SEE ANY-THING ELSE.
PAPA!
HERE COMES THE THREE-PART STOMP!
I DON'T CARE WHERE YOU HAVE TO DO IT!
ZUDOO (THADOOM)
JUST HIT HIM...
...WITH ANY-THING YOU CAN!

BACHI (CRACKLE)
I TOO...
BACHI
BACHI
...SHALL FIGHT!
BAO (BAZOOM)
BA (BZAK)
BA
NRRRN!
THERE YOU GO!
IT'S WORK-ING!
BA
BA
AH, YES... I KNEW MY BELOVED FREYJA-SAMA WOULD COME THROUGH FOR US...
YEAH, YEAH.

NUUUUUU (RUMBLE)
BWAH!
YOU LITTLE BUGS STRUGGLE MIGHTILY...
PERHAPS IT IS TIME FOR THE KING'S GLORY...
...TO BE POUNDED INTO YOUR SPINDLY BONES!
Thrym
Hp

HE'S CHANGING PATTERNS!
WATCH OUT!
HEY!
THIS IS BAD, ONII-CHAN.

THERE ARE ONLY THREE LIGHTS LEFT ON THE MEDALLION.
WE'VE PROBABLY GOT ONLY FIFTEEN MINUTES.
...!

HOW DO WE BEAT HIM... ... IN JUST FIFTEEN MINUTES?
BWAH-HAH-HAH! WHAT'S WRONG?
NIYARI (SMIRK)
AREN'T YOU GOING TO ATTACK?

THEN IT IS MY TURN!
FEEL THE ICY BREATH...
...OF THE KING OF THE FROST GIANTS!!
ZUOOOO (ZWOOSH)
GOOOOO (WHOOSH)
WHOA...!? WHAT'S THIS!?
W-WE'RE BEING SUCKED TOWARD HIM!
OOOO (WOOO)
I CAN USE WIND MAGIC TO CANCEL OUT THE SUCTION...!
GOTTA HURRY...
...BEFORE THE ATTACK HITS!
NEVER MIND!
THERE'S NO TIME!
LEAFA!
EVERY-ONE!
DEFEN-SIVE POSI-TIONS!!
BYUOOO (HOWL)

GOA (GWOOH)
...!
!!
BYUOOOOO
PIKI (CRAK)
PIKI
PIKI

UGH ...!
BWAH HAH HAH!
ZUOOO (LOOM)
NOW IS WHEN I CRUSH YOU TO DUST...
GIRARI (GLARE)
...LITTLE BUGS!!!

CHAPTER 5
GRR...!
GUOOOO (FWOOSH)
UUUAAAH!!
-OOOO- (WHOOSH)
THIS IS...
I... I CAN'T MOVE!
...REALLY BAD NEWS!!
PAAA (GLOW)
......!!

MAAAAAAAA
DOON (KABOOM)
AAH!!

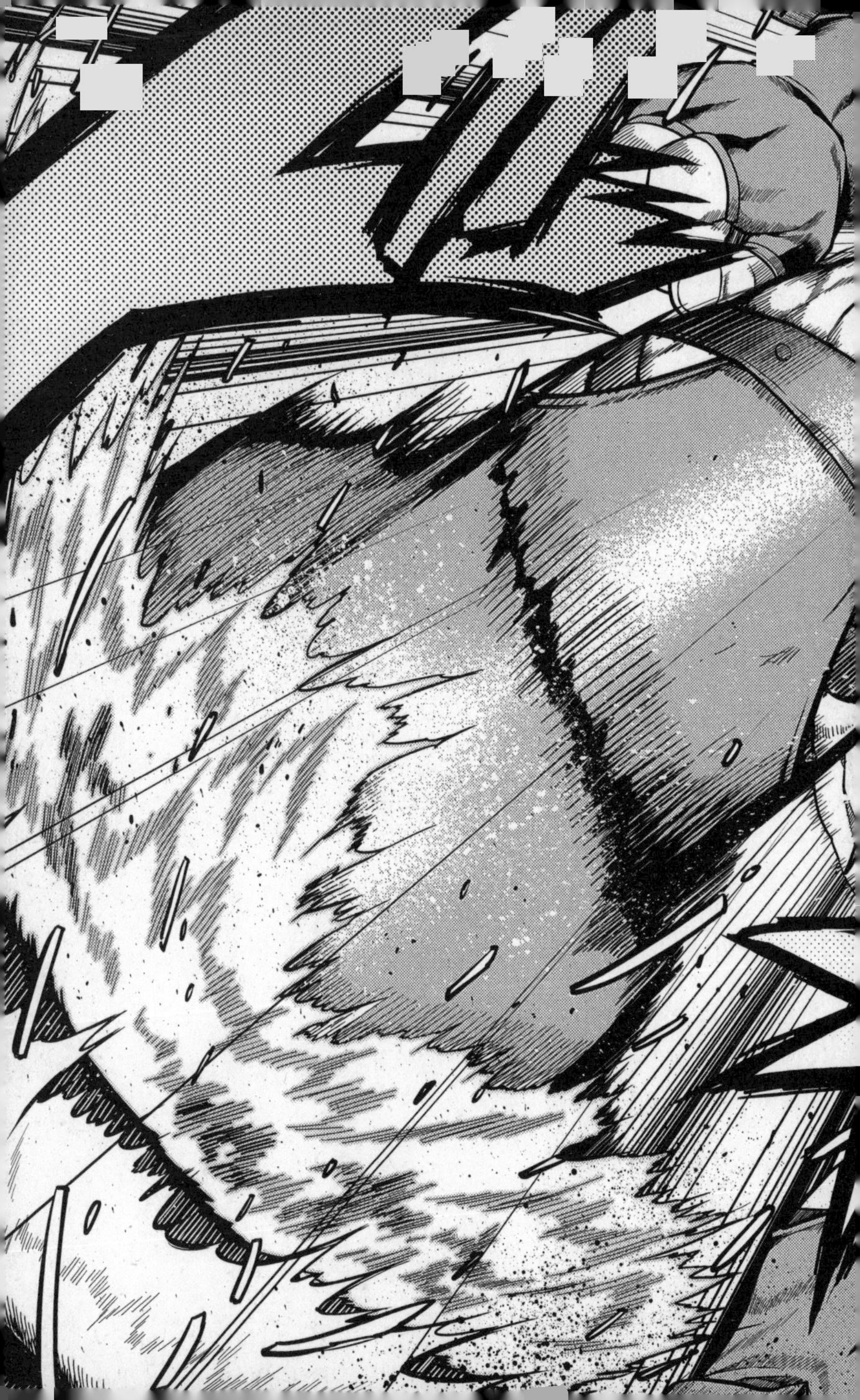

BA (BASH)
Kirito
Hp
Mp
Klein
Hp
Mp
Leafa
Hp
Mp
Silica
Hp
Mp
Lisbeth
Hp
Mp
BASHAAAN (KERSMASH)
BA

GA (THWAM)
!
-GA
OOOO (WHOOOH)
!!
H-HEY, WHERE'S SILICA?
SHUUUUU (FSHHH)
KYUU.
KYU...
KYUU.
OH, GOOD... PINA...
THE GUARD SKILL WORKED IN TIME...
KYUU.
PAAAA (SHINE)
WHAT?
PHEW...

ASUNA!
SHUOOO (WHOOSH)
SHE SAW THAT HEAVY DAMAGE COMING...
...AND PRE-CAST A PARTY-WIDE HEALING SPELL!
GUGU (STRAIN)
GRRR! LITTLE RUNTS!
THIS TIME I SHALL FINISH YOU...
ZUUN (ZMMF)
...WITH ONE MIGHTY...

...BLOW—
BOBOBOO (BABOOM)

TA
(TEP)
JA
(SHIK)
BOOOOO
(FWOOM)
MRRRR
RRNG!!
GAAAH!
BAAN
(THWAN)

トッ
TO (TUT)
KIRI (SWISH)
KIRI
NUUUU (CLOOM)
チラッ
CHIRA (GLANCE)
!
HRRRM!
KIRI
KIRI
GO
GO (RUMBLE)
SUCHA (SHWIK)
GO

INSOLENCE!
BUO (WHOOSH)
SINON!
GOOOOOO (ROAR)
GIVE US THIRTY SECONDS!
NI (GRIN)
ニッ

BO (WHOOM)
TA (TEK)
!!
OOOOOO
HE ATTACKS FASTER THAN I EXPECTED ...
...BUT IF I CLING TO HIS BODY AND FOCUS ON EVASION ...
HYUN (SWISH)
SINON-SAN!
YUI-CHAN!?

PAPA AND THE REST ARE RECOV-ERING.
IF ONLY THERE WERE PET HEALING POTIONS...
SO I'LL DO MY BEST TO HELP YOU OUT!
POSO (WHISPER)
"PAPA," HUH...?
?
GOOOOO (WHOOSH)
NEVER MIND. I'D WELCOME THE HELP.
OKAY!
WELL, HERE HE COMES!
NKKRAA
AA
AA
AA!!
DO (BOOM)
DO
A COMBO AT THAT SIZE!?
DO
I BELIEVE THAT'S A REACTION FOR WHEN SMALLER TARGETS CLIMB HIM!
THE AIMING IS WILD, BUT IT'S CONTINU-OUS...
...SO THERE'S LESS THAN A SECOND TO PREDICT HIS ATTACK!
DO
DO

ONE SECOND?
HEH!
FIVE RIGHT PUNCHES FROM 2 O'CLOCK!
TEN-METER INTERVAL!
THAT'S PLENTY MORE TIME THAN A BULLET GIVES YOU.
DO
LEFT, RIGHT!
DO
DODGE THE FOURTH RIGHT!
ONE SECOND!
DO
DO
TA (TEK)
NEXT!
BUN (WHOOSH)
HIS LEFT PALM...
WANT ME TO PREDICT IT?
HUH?
FROM *THIS ANGLE*...

BETWEEN THE MIDDLE AND RING FINGER ...
... RIGHT UP TO HIS FACE.
B-BUT IF YOU GET IN HIS FACE...
...HE'LL LAUNCH HIS ICE BREATH—!
GOOOOOOO (WHOOOOSH)
THAT'S OKAY.
IT'S BEEN THIRTY SECONDS.
OH.
KIRI (CRICK)
LET'S HEAD BACK.

OOO (ZWOOSH)
TA (TEK)
TA
TAN (TMP)
AND A ONE, AND A...
WAY TO GO, SINON-SAN!♡
WAAAA (CHEER)
WOW!!
GOOD JOB, SINON-SAN!
SAME TO YOU, YUI-CHAN.
NICE BACK-UP.
......OKAY.
Kirito
Klein
Leafa
Silica
Lisbeth
Sinon
Hp
Mp
!
...PREPARE TO ATTACK...
SIR SWORDSMAN.

NUUOOOO (RUMBLE)
AT THIS RATE...
...WE CANNOT DEFEAT THRYM.
Thrym Hp
OUR ONLY HOPE...
OO (WHOO)
...
OOO
...IS THE TREASURE OF MY PEOPLE...
...BURIED SOMEWHERE IN THIS CHAMBER.

SWORD
ART
ONLINE
—calibur—

CHAPTER 6

FREY-JA'S...
OOOO (WHOOOSH)
...TRUE POWER?
BO (BOOM)
...I SEE YOUR POINT.
OOO
WHAT ARE WE LOOKING FOR?
IT'S ABOUT THIS SIZE.
A GOLDEN HAMMER.

... HUH?

A...

A HAMMER?

A HAM-MER.

IT'S ABOUT THIS SIZE.

WHERE ARE YOUUU?

WHO DARES SHOOT ...

GUOOOO (ROAR)

...AN ARROW IN THE FACE OF THE KIIING?

THERE YOU ARE!

DOON (BOOM)

LITTLE WILD-CAT!!!

DO (BOOM)
...!
DO
DO
HE IGNORED THE FRONT LINE TO GO AFTER SINON-SAN!?
THE OLD MAN'S PRETTY FIXATED!
...HEY! KIRI, MY MAN!
GO BACK HER UP!
I'LL CATCH UP WITH YOU IN NO TIME!
OOOOO (ROAR)
YOU BET!
HEY! OVER HERE, BEARDO!

YAAAAAA
DO (RUSH)
DO
DO
AAH!!
DO
AAH!!
OOOO (ROAR)
RUAAAA!
GOTTA HURRY...
NEED TO FIND THIS THING FAST!
BUT HOW...
...AM I SUPPOSED TO FIND ONE LITTLE HAMMER...
...IN THIS GIGANTIC TREASURE ROOM...?
GOOOOOO (FWOOOSH)
YUI?
IT'S NOT THAT EASY, PAPA.
MY MAP DATA DOESN'T INCLUDE THE LOCATION OF KEY ITEMS.

I BELIEVE IT WAS PROBABLY RANDOMLY GENERATED WHEN WE ENTERED THE ROOM.
THE ONLY WAY TO DETERMINE WHICH ONE IS THE KEY...
...IS TO GIVE IT TO FREYJA-SAN!
GREAT...
GUESS I'LL JUST HAVE TO LOOK...
...IN EACH PILE...
ONII-CHAN!
USE A LIGHTNING TYPE SKILL!
HURRY!
DO
DO
DO
DO
L...
LIGHTNING...?
...!
SUCHA (SWISH)
OOO
OO

DA
(STOMP)
SEYAAAA!!
BAN
(LEAP)
AAAA!
LIGHTNING...
BAO
(BZAOW)
...FALL!!
BA
(BZZ)
BARI
(BZZT)
BARI
BACHII
(BZAP)
BARI
BA
BARII
BARI

...!
BA
BA
BACHIII
!!
PAPA!
I SAW IT!
TA (TEP)
DO (BOOM)
AAAH!
YAAAH!
DO
DON
DOOOO (KABOOM)
GAH ...

GA (LIFT)
HRNG!
AHH!
NOPE... NOT THAT!
GASHAN (CLANK)
POI (TOSS)
DYAH!
POI
OH!
NOT THAT EI- THER!
GACHA (CHUNK)
KIRA (SPARKLE)
......IS THIS IT!?
ZUSHI (DRAG)
!?
IT'S SO HEAVY ...!?
MERI (SLIP)
...NO TIME TO WASTE!
BUT...
GUN (STRAIN)

FREYJA-SAN!
HERE!
BUN (WHOOSH)
...OH, SHOOT!
I THREW IT AT FULL STRENGTH!
WHAT IF IT HITS HER...?
WILL I GET FLAGGED FOR ATTACKING AN NPC?
PASHI (SMACK)

HYURURU (SHWIPP)
PI (PAUSE)
SU (SWISH)
OOOO (WHOOSH)

........ING........
BACHI (ZAP)
...?
...FLOWING...
BACHI
BACHI
BACHI
BACHII
GOOOOOO (WHOOOM)
I AM OVER-FLOW-ING ......!
BACHI
BACHII
OOOO

I AM OVER-FLOW-ING...
KA (FLASH)
DOOON (BOOM)
...WITH POWER !!!
!!

BACHI (BZAT)
MEKI (CRAKLE)
DON
MEKI
DON
HMPH!
GRRRR!
BAN (BWAM)

BARI
(BZZT)
VUOO
(VWMMM)

SHE'S ......
...AN OLD DUDE !!
OOOOOOO (WHOOSH)

Asuna
Hp
Mp
Hp
Mp
BYUIIIN (BWEEE)
Thor
Hp
JI (ZZZT)
SAY, LEAFA, IS THAT ...?
YEAH... EXACTLY WHAT IT LOOKS LIKE, I SUSPECT.
THE FAMED NORSE FIGURE.
NUUUUU (GROWL)
THAT IS...
...THOR, GOD OF THUNDER!

COWARDLY GIANT!
NUUOO (GROWL)
YOU SHALL NOW PAY...
DOOOO (VOOM)
...FOR THE THEFT OF MY PRECIOUS MJOLNIR!
TREACHEROUS GOD!
PIKI (CRIK)
PAKI (CRAK)
GAFUUUUU (GWOO)
PIKI
GIRI (CLENCH)
YOU WILL RUE THIS DEVIANT LIE!

OOO (ROAR)
I WILL CUT OFF YOUR BEARD...
...AND SEND IT BACK TO ASGARD WHEN I'M DONE WITH YOU!

GAAN
(THWAM)

GOO (WHOOSH)
...!
...
...SAN.
FREYJAI-SAN.
OLD DUDE.
FREYJAI-SAN.
OLD DUDE.
FREYJA-SAN.
OLD DUDE ...

HEY, EVERY-ONE!
WHILE THOR'S HOLDING HIS ATTEN-TION...
...WE SHOULD ATTACK!
!!
YEAH!
ALL-OUT ATTACK!

USE ALL THE SWORD SKILLS YOU CAN!
LET'S GOOO !!!
DA (LEAP)

CHAPTER 7
GIRIII (STRAIN)
... HERE WE GO!
OOOO (WHOOSH)
BREAK HIS BALANCE FIRST!
FOCUSED ASSAULT !!

YAAAA!
HAH!!
GA
GA
GA
GA (GAK)
GRRG!
LITTLE BUGS ...!
DAMN!
GYARIN (KASHING)
GA
GA
GA

TAAAA!!
DON (BOOM)
DO
DO
DO
EVEN A GIANT IS WEAK...
...AT THE ACHILLES TENDON!
ZUGA (ZABLAM)
GA
GA
GA
GA

GOSU (WHOMP)
HEH-HEH! WHAT'S... ANOTHER GOOD WEAK SPOT?
LET'S TRY—
THE PINKIE!
ZAGAA (ZGASH)
THAT'S IT!
KEEP ATTACK...
...ING ......
ZA (STRIDE)

AND SO I HAVE TO HELP HER TO THE END.
THAT IS MY SAMURAI CODE—!
I DON'T CONSIDER THIS...
...A BETRAYAL OF MY SENTI-MENTS.
CHAKI (SHING)
I DECIDED TO FALL IN LOVE WITH A GODDESS.

JIWA (TEAR)
...IT'S NOT FAIR.
IT'S NOT...
KIIN (SHING)
...FAAAAIRR!!
BO (SLAM)

WAY TO GO!
HUH?
THRYM...IS STUNNED!
HRRNG...
ZUUOOO (ZWUMM)
NICE FORM ON THAT SLICE!
OW!
BAN (WHAP)
THAT'S IT!
PILE IT ON!!

EVERY-ONE CHARGE!
LET'S TAKE HIM DOWN!!
あ

DAAAAA
(DASH)
!

HRRGG!!
GOGOGO (ROAR)

DOO (BOOM)
YEAH!
NO...
NOT YET!
CURSE YOU... LITTLE BUGS!
NUOOO (GROWL)
YOU WILL PAY ......

GO
GO
...FOR THIS INSO-LENCE...
...WITH YOUR DEATHS!
GO (RUMBLE)
NUOOO
MAY YOU FREEZE...
...UNDER ETERNAL ICE—
AAH!!

DO
(THWAM)
DO
DOO
DO

GO (RUMBLE)
GO
GO
I SHALL FINISH YOU...
...WITH MY OWN TWO HANDS!
GRRR! DON'T GET FULL OF YOURSELF, THUNDER BOY!
RETURN TO THE DIRT FROM WHENCE YOU CAME...
...KING OF GIANTS!!
MAKE ME!!

THOR

PARI (PLINK)
Thrym
Hp
OOO (RUMBLE)

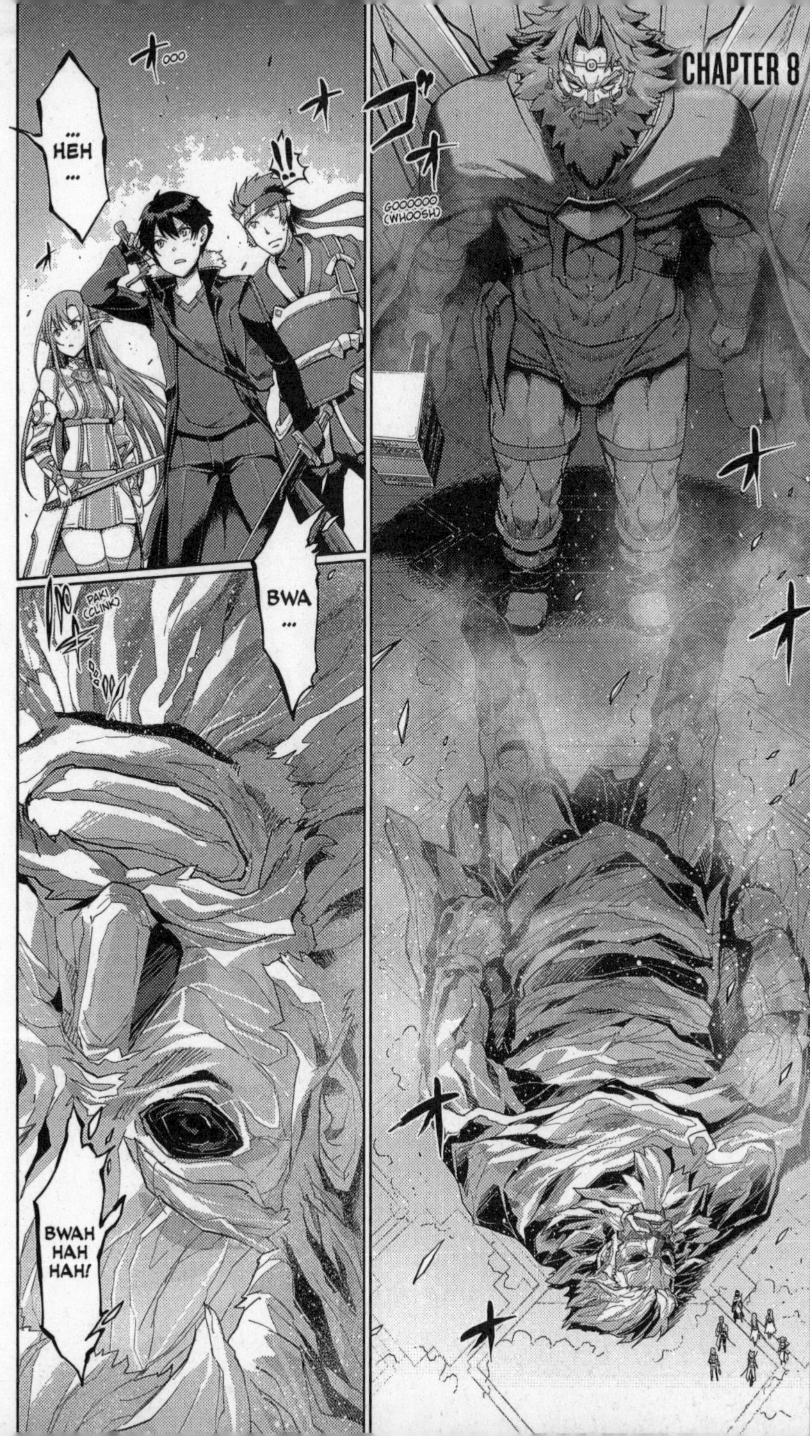
CHAPTER 8
GOOOOOO (WHOOSH)
...HEH...
BWA...
PAKI (CLINK)
BWAH HAH HAH!

ENJOY YOUR TRIUMPH, LITTLE BUGS.
NUOOOO (GROWL)
BUT YOU WILL SEE ......
YOU WILL RE-GRET ...
OOO (LOOM)
... TRUSTING THE AESIR ......
FOR THEY ARE...
...THE TRUE...
...PL—
ZUMU (STOMP)

BO (BOOM)
BON
BO
BO
DOO (KABOOM)
UH...

BARA (CLUNK)
BARA
DO (DSHH)
BARA
...FAIRY WAR-RIORS...
...YOU HAVE MY THANKS.
GOOOOOOOO (WHOOSHH)
...YOU MUST HAVE...
...A FITTING REWARD.
I HAVE REGAINED MY HONOR...
...AFTER THE SHAME OF LOSING MY TREASURE.
BASHU (BSHK)
KIRA (GLINT)

PARI (CRAKK)
USE MJOLNIR, HAMMER OF LIGHT-NING...
BACHI (ZAP)
OOF...
ZUSHI (HEFT)
...FOR YOUR RIGHTEOUS BATTLES.
BACHI
AND NOW... FARE-WELL.
BACHI

DOON (BOOM)
KA (FLASH)
...!
PARI (PRIK)
OOON (OOOM)
BACHI (ZZAT)

PA (POP)
PARI
PARI
PA
PA
BUWA (BWOOF)
STATIC?
KYU?
PA
WELL, THERE ARE THE BOSS REWARDS...
RESULT
Soldier's Helm
Dwarven Ma
Sharp Nil
Azure Cryst
Wiltooth
Mercury Da
Nocteshtra
...SO I GUESS WE WON...?
ピローン
PIROOON (BLING)
FUU (RELIEF)
BURU (SHIVER)
ACK!
BURU BURU
KLEIN.
PON (PAT)
CONGRATS ON THE LEGENDARY WEAPON.
......AND HERE I AM, WITHOUT A SINGLE POINT IN HAMMER SKILLS.
WELL, I'M SURE LIZ WOULD BE HAPPY TO TAKE IT OFF YOUR HANDS.

OH WAIT, SHE'LL PROBABLY MELT IT DOWN FOR INGOTS ......
CHIRA (GLANCE)
HEY!
EVEN I WOULDN'T BE THAT WASTE-FUL!
AH!
BUT, LIZ...
I HEAR YOU GET AN INCREDIBLE NUMBER OF ORICHALCUM INGOTS IF YOU MELT DOWN A LEGENDARY!
I NEVER THOUGHT OF THAT!
WHAT, REALLY?
HEH!
DAKI (SQUEEZE)
H-HEY! I HAVEN'T SAID I'M GIVING IT TO YOU YET!
HEE!
PUT DOWN THE HAMMER!
NOOO!
HEE!
HA HA!
AH HA HA HA HA
HA
HA HA!
H-HEH...

HA
HA
HA!
(HA-HA!)
HA!
ZU (ZMMM)
ZU
!
ZUN (ZMMM)
WHOA!
AAAAH!
WE'RE...... MOVING!?
NO...
GO (RUMBLE)
GO
GO
THE CASTLE THRYM-HEIM...
...IS FLOATING ......!
O...... ONII-CHAN! THE QUEST IS STILL GOING!!
GO
GO
GO
GO

GO (RUMBLE)
GO
WH-WHAT!?
DIDN'T WE BEAT THAT GIANT DUDE!?
GO
GO
ACTUALLY... URD, QUEEN OF THE LAKE, TOLD US...
...WE NEEDED TO INFILTRATE THRYM-HEIM...
...AND DRAW EXCALIBUR FROM THE PEDESTAL.
TH- THE LAST LIGHT IS BLINKING!
IF THIS VANISHES, THAT MEANS ALL OF THE KINDRED BEASTS ARE DEAD—
GYU (SQUEEZE)
OH, TONKY...!!
PAPA!
THERE'S A DOWNWARD STAIRCASE BEING GENERATED BEHIND THE THRONE!
...!!
DA (DASH)

...I CAN'T IMAGINE IT PUSHING SUCH A RIDICULOUS STORY ARC THROUGH......

LISTEN, ONII-CHAN.

I ONLY REMEMBER A FEW VAGUE DETAILS......

...BUT I'M PRETTY SURE THAT IN THE ORIGINAL MYTH...

...THRYM WASN'T ACTUALLY THE MASTER OF THRYMHEIM CASTLE.

UH... WHAT!? BUT THE NAME...

YEAH, I KNOW.
BUT IN THE NORSE MYTH, IT WAS... TH...... TH......
THJAZI!
YES!
IN THE MYTH IT WAS NOT THRYM WHO DESIRED URD'S GOLDEN APPLE...
...BUT ANOTHER FIGURE NAMED THJAZI.

WITHIN ALO...
...IT SEEMS THE NPC OFFERING THE SLAUGHTER QUEST...
...IS LOCATED IN THE LARGEST CASTLE DOWN IN JOTUNHEIM...
...AND HIS NAME IS ARCHDUKE THJAZI.

SO IF THRYMHEIM ASCENDS TO ALNE, EVEN WITHOUT THRYM IN IT...
...THIS ARCHDUKE THJAZI WILL TAKE OVER AND LEAD THE ATTACK ON ALFHEIM...
...MEANING THE REPLACEMENT'S ALWAYS BEEN THERE FROM THE START......

HEY, WE KNEW IT WOULDN'T BE A WALK IN THE PARK!

......PAPA, FIVE SECONDS UNTIL THE EXIT!
DA (STOMP)
DA
OKAY!
DA

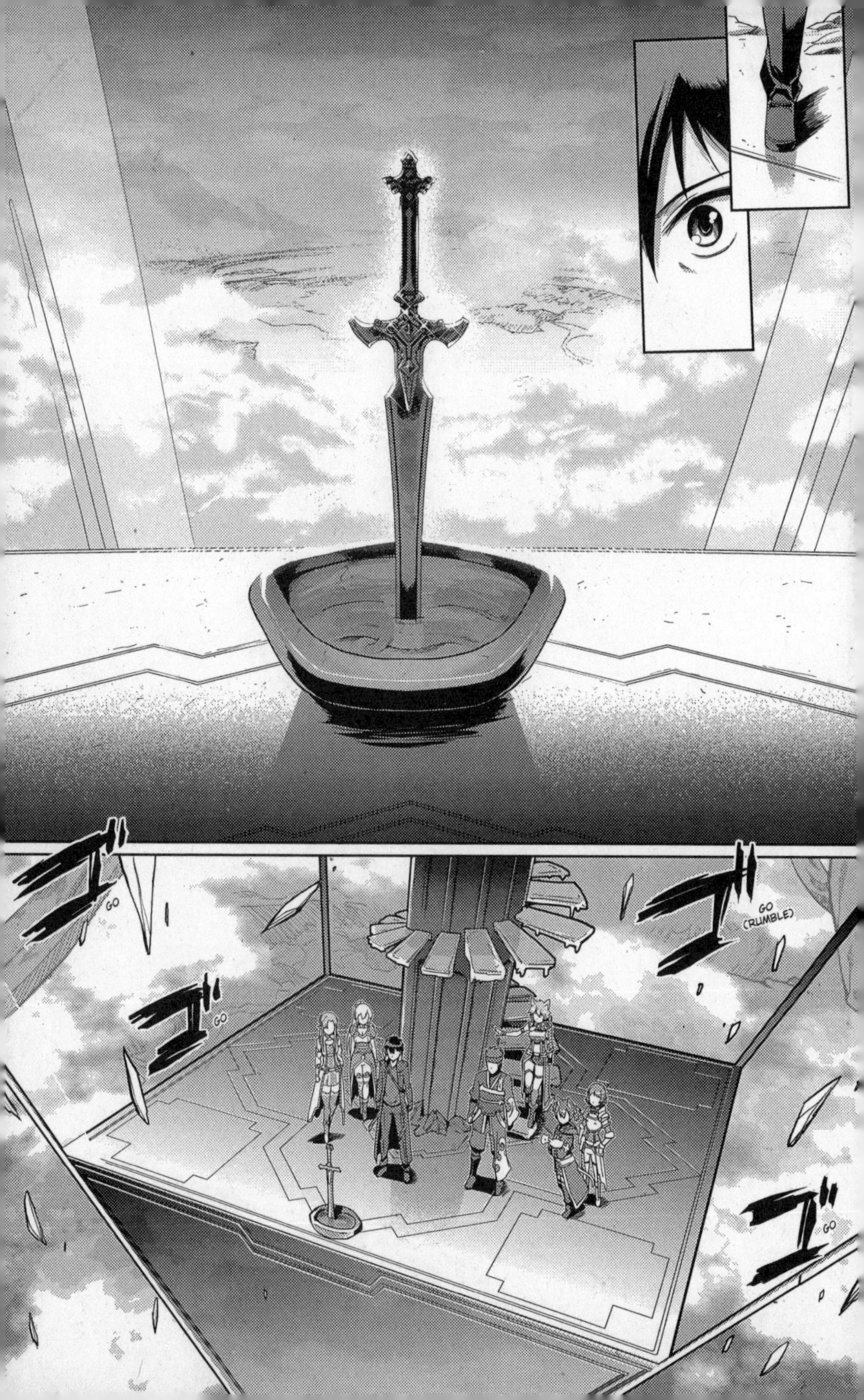
GO
(RUMBLE)
GO
GO
GO

ゴ GO
HERE WE ARE...
ゴ GO
ゴ GO
ゴ GO (RUMBLE)
MADE IT AT LAST...
System Command!! Generate Object ID...
...Excalibur!!

BACK THEN, I CREATED THE WORLD'S STRONGEST SWORD WITH A SINGLE SPOKEN COMMAND.
IT WASN'T RIGHT. IT WAS CHEATING.
BUT NOW...
THIS TIME ......
SORRY ABOUT THE WAIT.
GU (CLENCH)

HRNG!
GISHI (CREAK)
GAH!
WH-WHAT THE HELL IS THIS...?
IT'S NOT... BUDGING...!
ぎしーッ
GISHI
BURU (SHAKE)
ぶるぶるッ
BURU
GU (STRAIN)
GU
KEEP TRYING!
YOU CAN DO IT, KIRITO-KUN!
ARRGH!
GU

KRU-RU!
YOU CAN DO IT!
YOU CAN DO IT!
SHOW US WHAT YOU'VE GOT!
YOU CAN DO IT!
YOU CAN DO IT!
C'MON, ALMOST THERE!
YOU CAN DO IT, PAPA!
AH...

THAT WAS... IT......
... RIGHT ...?
!
PIKI (CRAKK)
キッ
—HEY, KIRI!
SOME-THING'S WRONG! LOOK AT THE PLINTH ......!
MEKI (CRIK)
めきっ
MEKI
GOPA (GRUKK)
THERE ARE ROOTS!

BOGOO
(GRUNCH)

CHAPTER 9
DO
DO (BAM)
DO
DO
DO
GO (RUMBLE)
GO
IT'S GONNA SPLIT APART......!
GO
GO
WH-WHOA!? IT......
GO
GO
GO
THRYM-HEIM ITSELF IS COLLAPS-ING!
WE MUST ESCAPE, PAPA!
YEAH, BUT...
...NO STAIRS!
GO
GO
GO

GO
GO
HEY, WORLD TREE!
THIS ISN'T VERY THOUGHT-FUL OF YOU!
WHY ARE YOU YELLING AT THE TREE?
DARN YOU!
YEAH!
GO
GO (RUMBLE)
GO
AND WE CAN'T JUMP TO THE ROOTS...
IT'S TOO FAR.
AND WE CAN'T JUMP DOWN. WE'LL EITHER HIT THE GROUND OR LAND IN THE GREAT VOID.
GO
WE'LL DIE!
SURE WILL.
AW-RIGHT ......!
GO
GO
TIME TO CHECK OUT THE GREAT KLEIN-SAMA'S MEDAL-WINNING HIGH-JUMP SKILLS—!
NO, YOU IDIOT, DON'T—
DA (DASH)
CHECK THIS OUT!
② SOME-THING TO GRAB?
① JUMP SUPER HIGH

PISHI (CRIK)
PIKI
PIKI (CRAK)
PAKI (CREAK)

DO
(CRUMBLE)
DO
DO
DO
DO
DO
!......!!
GOOOO
(WHOOSH)
K......
KLEIN-
SAN—
MOU IDIOOOOOOT!!
GOO
BARA
(CRUMBLE)
BARA
BARA

...I WONDER WHAT'S DOWN THERE.
MAYBE IT'S LIKE URD-SAN SAID...
...AND IT GOES ALL THE WAY DOWN TO NIFLHEIM!
GOOOOO
BYUOOO (VOOOM)
I HOPE IT'S NOT TOO COLD ......
U-UMM...
I BET IT'S FREEZING!
HA
HA
HA!
IT'S THE HOME OF THE FROST GIANTS!
OH! THAT REMINDS ME. LEAFA ...
HOW GOES THE SLAUGHTER QUEST?
!
GOKU (GULP)
SU (SWISH)

OH...
WE'RE STILL GOOD! ONE LIGHT LEFT!
WE MADE IT IN TIME...
BA (HUG)
WHOA!
...ONII-CHAN!
KYU (SQUEEZE)
I'M SO GLAD...!
BARA
BARA (CRUMBLE)
BARA
BARA
THE WORLD TREE IS REGAINING ITS FORMER POWER.
URD AND HER KINDRED BEASTS WILL BE ABLE TO RECOVER...
...AND THE HUMANOID DEVIANT GODS WILL STOP HUNTING THEM.
SO EVEN IF WE FALL TO OUR DEATHS HERE...
...OUR TEMPORARY SACRIFICE WILL BE WORTH IT.
CHIRA (GLANCE)

BII (BEEP)
ビーッ
UNAVAILABLE
聖剣エクスキャリバー
UNAVAILABLE
MENU: HOLY SWORD EXCALIBUR
NOPE, DOESN'T WORK.
I HAVE TO COMPLETE THE QUEST...
PI
ピッ
...BEFORE I CAN GAIN OWNERSHIP OF EXCALIBUR ......
HUH ...?
...I HEARD SOMETHING.
!
THAT WAS IT!
THERE IT IS AGAIN!
BYUOOO (WHOOSH)
H-HEY, BE CAREFUL!
KWOOOO...
!!

KWOOO!
...!!
TONKY !!
OVER HERE!
TH-THIS WAY, THIS WAAAY!
WA (SHOUT)
TONKY!
HEH HEH...I KNEW THIS WOULD HAPPEN...
HAR HAR...
KNEW THAT GUY WOULD COME AND SAVE US AT THE LAST SECOND ......
LIAR !!!!!!

FUWA (FLOAT)
KWOOO!
LET'S JUMP, GUYS!
C-CAN'T YOU GET ANY CLOSER?
♪
TO (TMP)

BA (HOP)
TRAAAH!!
FUWA (FLOAT)
TO (TMP)
YOU FIRST.
...
OOOO (WHOOSH)
GOKU (GULP)
A...
AW-RIGHT, GET READY...
...TO FEAST YOUR EYES...
...ON MY GRACEFUL ......
SUI (SHOVE)
OOO
...!!

SHURU (SHLIP)
!!
BUO (SWING)
OH MY GOD!!
KWOO!♥
...
S-STOP, TONKY! PUT ME DOWN!
WAAA (YELL)
OH NO...!
ZUSHI (HEFT)
...THAT I CAN'T EVEN JUMP...
...THE SHORT DISTANCE TO MY GOAL...
EXCALIBUR'S SO HEAVY...
KIRITO!
KIRITO-KUN!
PISHI (CRAK)
MISHI (CREAK)

SO I CAN EITHER FALL TO MY DEATH HOLDING EXCALIBUR OR DISCARD IT AND LIVE......
WHAT A DEVIOUS SET OF OPTIONS.
PAPA ...?
KON (DINK)
......
DAMN YOU ...
...CAR-DINAL!
BUN (FLING)

OOOO (WHOOSH)
FINAL CHAPTER
OOOO
TA (TEP)
...WE CAN GO BACK AND FIND IT SOME-TIME.
PON (PAT)
I'LL GET A LOCK ON ITS COORDI-NATES!

OO (WHOOSH)
YEAH... GOOD IDEA.
I'M SURE IT'LL BE WAITING FOR ME...
...SOME-WHERE IN NIFL-HEIM—
SU (SWISH)
JAKI (CHAK)
BARA (CRUMBLE)
BARA
BARA
BOSO (MURMUR)
TWO HUNDRED METERS...
Ek skýt aftur ör
FUON (FWOM)

THE "RETRIEVING ARROW" SPELL...?
SINON... YOU CAN'T.
EVEN YOU COULDN'T ...
GIRI (CRICK)
ONE.
THE STRING TIED TO THE ARROW MAKES ITS FLIGHT UNSTABLE...
TWO.
TWO HUNDRED METERS ...?
ONE ...
GOKU (GULP)
THAT'S NEARLY TWICE THE RANGE OF THE BOW I CRAFTED FOR HER, ISN'T IT?

KU (TIK)
KURU (SPIN)
ONE.
TSUI (SWISH)
TWO.
KURU
SUUU (EXHALE)
MM!
KIRI (CRICK)
BASHU (SHOOT)
HYUOO (WHOOSH)

GUN (TUG)
OO (WHOOSH)
ZUSHI (HEFT)
WHOA.
AH!
SO HEAVY ......
S......
......SINON-SAN......
S......
ZAWA (MURMUR)
ZAWA

WHOAAAA!
SINON-SAN'S SO FREAKIN' COOL!!!!!!
HMPH!
......
HEH!
DON'T LOOK SO PITIFUL. YOU CAN HAVE IT.
HERE.
TH... THANKS.
BUT FIRST... ...PROMISE ME ONE THING.

EVERY TIME YOU DRAW THIS SWORD ...
...I WANT YOU TO THINK OF ME.
DOOON (BOOM)
... ...
NYURU (BLOOP)
にゅるっ
OOOH.

MUST BE TOUGH...
...BEING A REAL PLAYER ...
GASU (STOMP)
GO (BAM)
MY!
MY PINKIE TOE!
...YES, I'LL THINK OF YOU. AND BE GRATEFUL.
THANK YOU. YOUR AIM WAS SIMPLY SUPERB.
YOU'RE WEL-COME.
PACHI (WINK)
ZUUUN (HEAVY)
HISO (WHISPER)
HISO
YIKES...
SPEAK-ING WITH THEIR EYES ...?
SHE WINKED AT HIM.
KIRITO-SAN...
ZAWA
ZAWA (MURMUR)
SHE...
SHE GOT ONE OVER ON ME...
SUPAAA (PUFF)
PEPPERMINT
PIKO (TWITCH)
PIKO

DO (RUMBLE)
DO
GOPA! (KRUNCH)
THERE GOES THRYM-HEIM...
DO
DO
KWOOO!
DO
DO
...SO WE GOT TO GO ON ONE LITTLE ADVEN-TURE...
DO
...AND NOW THAT DUNGEON'S GOING TO BE LOST FOREVER ......?
IT'S A BIT OF A SHAME, ISN'T IT?
THERE WERE PLENTY OF ROOMS WE DIDN'T EVEN GO IN...
DO
OUR MAPPING PERCENT-AGE WAS ONLY 37.2%.
DO
DO
DO

YEAH, IT'S A REAL WASTE.
DO
DO
BUT I HAD A LOTTA FUN.
......
SAY, LEAFA. SO, ERM...
THAT FREYJA'S STILL A REAL GODDESS SOMEWHERE, RIGHT?
ONE THAT AIN'T THOR IN DISGUISE?
OO (WHOOSH)
... YEAH.
THAT'S RIGHT.
OH, GREAT! SO IF I GO AROUND LOOKIN'...
...I MIGHT JUST MEET HER SOMEDAY!
OOO
...MAYBE.
UM, PAPA... ASGARD, HOME OF THE AESIR, DOESN'T EXIST IN ALO...
POSHO (WHISPER)
DON'T MENTION IT, YUI.
BUT... THRYM WAS SAYING SOMETHING AS HE DISINTEGRATED.
THAT THE AESIR WERE THE TRUE... SOMETHING...
WHOA, HEY! CHECK IT OUT!
THE GREAT VOID!
OOO

IT'S FILLING FROM BELOW ...
ZAAAA (FSHHH)
ZA
ZA
ZAN
DOZA (DWOOH)
THAT'S ... WATER, RIGHT?
ZAA
ZA
ZA
OH! KIRITO-KUN!
THAT'S RIGHT. SHE SAID THE GREAT VOID...
...USED TO BE A LAKE, BEFORE THRYM-HEIM ASCENDED HERE.
ZAAAAA
DOO (BOOM)
OH! LOOK UP!
AAAAAH!!

H-HEY, LOOK AT THAT!
ROOTS!
GOOO (VWOOM)
THE ROOTS OF THE WORLD TREE ......
ZAAN
DO (RUMBLE)
DO
MEKI (CRAK)
DO
DO
WOW...
MEKI
DO

OOO (WHOOSH)
LOOK AT THE ROOTS...
PON (POP)
PON
THEY'RE BUDDING...
BO
BO
!?
BO (BOMP)
!
PON
BO
BUWA (BWOOSH)
!!
WOOOW...!

KWOO!
KWOOOOH!
KWOO!
くぉっ♡
くぉっ
KWOO!
KWOOH!
くぉーん
KWOOOH!
くぉぉーん
くぉーっ
KWOOH!
くぉーんっ
KWOOH!
HA HA...
WHAT'S THIS...?

...I'M GLAD...
I'M SO GLAD FOR YOU, TONKY.
OOO (WHOOSH)
KWOO!
LOOK AT ALL THOSE FRIENDS!
KWOO!
THERE ...
...AND THERE ...
KWOO!
BORO (TEAR)
SO MANY FRIENDS ...
...ALL AROUND US...
OOO
GUSU (SNIFF)

YUI ...?
HUH?
...?
MAMA...
GYU (SQUEEZE)
YES.
I'M SO HAPPY FOR LEAFA AND TONKY TOO.
!!
!
YOU HAVE SUCCEEDED ...
...AND SUCCEEDED GLORIOUSLY.
FUOON (VWOOM)
WITH THE REMOVAL OF EXCALIBUR, BLADE THAT CUTS ALL STEEL AND WOOD...
...THE SPIRIT ROOT SEVERED FROM YGGDRASIL HAS RETURNED TO ITS MOTHER TREE.

THE TREE'S BLESSING FILLS THE LAND ONCE MORE...
...AND JOTUNHEIM HAS REGAINED ITS PROPER FORM.
THIS IS ALL THANKS TO YOU.
AWW...... SHUCKS.
IF IT WEREN'T FOR THOR...
...I DOUBT WE'D HAVE EVER BEATEN THRYM...
I FELT THE THUNDER GOD'S POWER AS WELL.
BUT...BE CAUTIOUS, FAIRIES.
THE AESIR MAY BE THE ENEMIES OF THE FROST GIANTS...
...BUT THAT DOES NOT MAKE THEM YOUR FRIENDS.
UM... THRYM WAS TRYING TO SAY SOMETHING LIKE THAT HIMSELF.
WHAT DOES IT...?
OOO (WHOOSH)
PAAAA (GLOW)
—MY SISTERS WISH...
...TO THANK YOU AS WELL.

FUOO (FWISH)
MY NAME IS VER-DANDI.
THANK YOU, FAIRY WAR-RIORS.
IT IS LIKE A DREAM TO WITNESS JOTUNHEIM GREEN AND VERDANT AGAIN......
MY NAME IS SKULD!
YOU HAVE MY THANKS, WAR-RIORS!

PAAA (GLOW)
N-NO! I WON'T!
HEE HEE!
AND WE SHALL GRANT YOU THAT BLADE.
BE CAREFUL NOT TO HURL IT INTO URD'S SPRING.
OH...
HYUUUU (WHOOSH)
WOW, LOOK AT ALL THESE REWARDS ...!
TEMPORARY S
PIROROROROO (BRRIIIIIING)
THIS IS GOING TO FILL ALL OF OUR ITEM STORAGE!
DOKI (BADUM)
DOKI
WA
WA (FRET)
PI (BEEP)
PI
PIROROROROO
PIROROROROO
PI
...
▶ Holy Sword Excalibur
...!
GU (CLENCH)

THANK YOU, FAIRIES.
MAY WE MEET AGAIN.
OH!
...!
FUOOOO (FWISH)
DA (DASH)
Holy Sword of the Ice Labyrinth
氷宮の聖剣
Quest Clear
JAAAN (TADAAA)

S...S... SKULD-SAN!
WHAT!?
HOW CAN I GET IN TOUCH WITH YOU!?
ARE YOU KIDDING ME!?
WHAT ABOUT YOU AND FREYJA-SAN!?
AN NPC ISN'T GONNA GIVE YOU HER PHONE NUMBER!!
HEH HEH.
KIRA (GLINT)
HIRA (SWISH)
HUH?
...SHE SMILED?

キラ KIRA
...
KIRA キラ
KLEIN, AT THIS VERY MOMENT ...
KIRA キラ
KIRA キラ
...YOU HAVE MY UTMOST RESPECT.
キラ KIRA
...HEY, GUYS ...
FEEL LIKE A PARTY AND YEAR-END CELEBRATION?
I'M IN.
OHHH! SKULD-SAMA!
ME TOO!
KWOOO!

SIGN: RESERVED FOR THE DAY
Dicey Cafe.
...WHAT IS THAT?
HOW'S THIS, YUI?
I can see.
I can see and hear... ... every-thing, Papa!
OKAY, TRY SOME SLOW MOVEMENT.
JUIN (ZWEE)
Sure!
AH, I SEE.
SO THOSE CAMERAS AND MICS ARE LIKE YUI-CHAN'S OWN INPUTS ......
HER SENSORY ORGANS.
VIEW :Yui

AT SCHOOL, ONII-CHAN'S IN THE MECHA...... MECHA-TON......
MECHA-TRONICS.
...THAT-NICS ELECTIVE COURSE, SO HE BUILT THEM FOR CLASS CREDIT.
BUT IT'S REALLY JUST FOR YUI-CHAN!
TADA!
I can keep ordering more food!
PHEW...
HEE HEE!
SORRY, AGIL!
AH HA HA!
TH-THAT'S NOT ALL! IF I CAN SHRINK THE CAMERA DOWN AND MOUNT IT ON A SHOULDER OR HEAD...
...THEN WE CAN TAKE THE MACHINE ANY-WHERE...
AND THAT'S FOR YUI-CHAN TOO, I'M SAYING!
カラーン
KARAAAN (CLINK)
HEY, EVERY-ONE.
'SUP!
OH, LOOKS LIKE WE'RE ALL HERE!

ALL RIGHT! AND NOW...
...A TOAST.
TO EARNING EXCALIBUR...
SO LONG, 2025!
...AND MJOLNIR!
CHEERS!
かんぱーいっ
KANPAAAI (CHEERS)

...I'VE BEEN WONDERING...
...YOU KNOW.
WHY IS IT "EXCALIBUR"?

HUH? WHAT DO YOU MEAN?
NORMALLY IN FANTASY NOVELS AND MANGA AND STUFF...
...WE JAPANESE PRONOUNCE IT MORE LIKE "EXCULL-IBER."
OH, THAT'S WHAT YOU'RE TALKING ABOUT.
KURU (TWIRL)
KURU
OOOH, YOU READ THOSE BOOKS, SINON-SAN?
I PRACTICALLY OWNED THE LIBRARY IN MIDDLE SCHOOL.

I THINK THERE WERE SEVERAL MORE NAMES IN THE ORIGINAL LEGEND.
REMEMBER HOW, IN THE QUEST, THERE WAS A FAKE VERSION CALLED CALIBURN?
THAT WAS ONE OF THE REAL NAMES IN THAT LIST, I'M PRETTY SURE.
The main variations...
...are Caledfwlch, Caliburnus, Calesvol...
...Collbrande, Caliburn, and Escalibor, depending on the language.
Excalibur
SHEESH, THERE ARE THAT MANY?

WELL, IT DOESN'T MEAN MUCH. IT JUST STRUCK ME AS INTERESTING...
...SINCE "CALIBER" HAS A VERY SPECIFIC MEANING TO ME.
HUH? WHAT'S THAT?
CALIBER IS THE ENGLISH WORD FOR A BULLET'S SIZE.
MY HECATE II IS A "FIFTY CALIBER" BECAUSE ITS ROUNDS ARE .50 INCHES WIDE.
I THINK THE ENGLISH SPELLING IS DIFFERENT FROM EXCALIBUR, THOUGH.
BUT IT CAN ALSO REFER...
...TO A PERSON'S QUALITY OF CHARACTER.
IT'S WHY "A MAN OF HIGH CALIBER"...
...MEANS SOMEONE OF GREAT QUALITY.
OOH, I NEED TO REMEMBER THAT.
IT PROBABLY WON'T COME UP ON ANY TESTS.
IN THAT CASE...
DON (SLAM)
...I GUESS THEY NEEDED TO MAKE SURE EXCALIBUR'S OWNER...
...HAD THE PROPER CALIBER.
UH...

FROM WHAT I'VE HEARD DOWN THE GRAPE-VINE...
...A CERTAIN SOMEONE MADE QUITE A KILLING WITH A SHORT-TERM JOB RECENTLY!
URK...
OF...
OF COURSE I INTENDED ...
...TO PAY FOR TODAY'S PARTY...
DON (THUMP)
...ALL ALONG! YOU KNOW THAT!
HYUUU (FWEEET)
PACHI (CLAP)
PACHI
WAA (CHEER)
PACHI
PACHI
PACHI
PACHI
Let's put in an order for more food, Papa!
IT'S SO FUN...
...TO HELP OUT!
WAIT. UM...YUI? HANG ON A SECOND!
AH-HA-HA-HA-HA-HA!

SWORD ART ONLINE.
GUN GALE ONLINE.
ALF-HEIM ONLINE.
IF THERE'S ONE THING I'VE LEARNED ...
...ABOUT HUMAN POTENTIAL THROUGH MY JOURNEYS HERE...
...IT'S THAT A SINGLE MAN CANNOT SUPPORT ANYTHING ON HIS OWN.
IN EACH WORLD, I WAS BROUGHT TO MY KNEES MANY TIMES ...
...AND WAS ONLY ABLE TO CARRY ON THANKS TO THE HELP OF OTHERS.
TODAY'S SPONTA-NEOUS ADVENTURE IS THE PERFECT EXAMPLE OF THAT.

SO I'M CERTAIN THAT MY CALIBER ...
...NO, OUR CALIBER —
—IS AS WIDE AS THE CIRCLE OUR GROUP MAKES WHEN WE STAND HAND IN HAND.
I WILL NOT USE THAT GOLDEN SWORD...
...FOR JUST MY OWN GAIN.

がばっ
GABA (GRAB)
C'MON, ANOTHER TOAST!
WE JUST DID THAT.
WHAT'S THIS ONE FOR?
ISN'T IT OBVIOUS?
TO THE GROUP'S CALIBER!
......
YEAH.
CHEERS!
fin.

HELLO, THIS IS CSY.
LIKE THE QUEST IN *CALIBUR*, DRAWING THIS STORY WAS A VERY TOUGH BUT REWARDING JOURNEY.
IT'S A SHORT STORY BUT ONE PACKED WITH INFORMATION, SO I WENT IN EXPECTING TO HAVE TO SINGLE OUT JUST THE IMPORTANT STUFF...UNTIL I GOT CARRIED AWAY WITH DRAWING KLEIN AND THRYM. YOU MAY NOTICE THAT WHEN SINON-SAN SHOWED UP, I THREW IN MORE BUTT ANGLES THAN USUAL (LOL).
ANYWAY, IT WAS FUN DRAWING THESE CHARACTERS. THEY'RE SO LIVELY THAT THEY KNOW WHAT TO DO EVEN WHEN THERE AREN'T LINES OF DIALOGUE TO FOLLOW. I HOPE THAT YOU READERS CAN FEEL THE ENJOYMENT FROM THE STORY, AS I DID.
THANK YOU ALL FOR READING!
KIYA SHII (CSY)

SWORD ART ONLINE CALIBUR

ART: SHII KIYA
ORIGINAL STORY: REKI KAWAHARA
CHARACTER DESIGN: abec

Translation: Stephen Paul
Lettering: Brndn Blakeslee & Katie Blakeslee

Edited by ASCII MEDIA WORKS
First published in Japan in 2015 by KADOKAWA CORPORATION, Tokyo.
English translation rights arranged with KADOKAWA CORPORATION, Tokyo, through Tuttle-Mori Agency, Inc., Tokyo.

Yen Press
1290 Avenue of the Americas
New York, NY 10104

Visit us at yenpress.com
facebook.com/yenpress
twitter.com/yenpress
yenpress.tumblr.com
instagram.com/yenpress

First Yen Press Edition: December 2017

Yen Press is an imprint of Yen Press, LLC.
The Yen Press name and logo are trademarks of Yen Press, LLC.

Library of Congress Control Number: 2017954643

ISBNs: 978-0-316-44256-5 (paperback)
978-0-316-44257-2 (ebook)

10 9 8 7 6 5 4 3 2 1

BVG

Printed in the United States of America